An Apple for Harriet Tubman

Glennette
Tilley Turner

Illustrated by **Susan Keeter**

Albert Whitman & Company, Morton Grove, Illinois

In memory of Mrs. Alice Brickler, Mrs. Caroline Rubin, and
Mrs. Evelyn Turner, and for Dr. A. D. Brickler, Ms. Alice Brickler, Mrs. Faye Daniels,
Mrs. Billie Bob, and the survivors of Hurricane Katrina.—G.T.T.

To my mother and my late stepfather, artists Carolyn Heery Berry
and Paul Snow Berry.—S.K.

*Harriet Tubman, in a photo
taken between 1860 and 1875.*

Library of Congress Cataloging-in-Publication Data

Turner, Glennette Tilley.
An apple for Harriet Tubman / by Glennette Tilley Turner ; illustrated by Susan Keeter.
p. cm.
ISBN-10: 0-8075-0395-9 (hardcover)
ISBN-13: 978-0-8075-0395-9 (hardcover)
1. Tubman, Harriet, 1820?-1913—Juvenile literature. 2. Slaves—United States—Biography—Juvenile literature.
3. African American women—Biography—Juvenile literature. 4. Underground railroad—Juvenile literature.
I. Keeter, Susan, ill. II. Title.
E444.T82T87 2006 973.7'115092—dc22 2005037360

The design is by Carol Gildar.

For more information about Albert Whitman & Company, please visit our web site at www.albertwhitman.com.

Harriet was born into slavery around the year 1820. Her parents, Ben and Rit Ross, were enslaved on the Brodess plantation in Maryland. Because their parents were the property of Edward Brodess, Harriet and her brothers and sisters belonged to him, too, the law said.

The slaves had a hard life. They chopped down trees, cleared swamps, tended the tobacco fields, and did all the other jobs on the Brodess plantation.
The slaves didn't get paid and had to do everything their overseers told them to do.
Even children had to work.

When Harriet was only seven, Edward Brodess sent her to work for an unkind woman named Miss Susan. One of Harriet's jobs was to sit up all night taking care of Miss Susan's baby so her crying would not wake her mother. If the baby did cry, Miss Susan would whip Harriet.

Later on, Harriet worked in the fields. She liked working outdoors where she could feel the fresh breezes, see the sunshine, and watch birds fly free.

Picking apples was her favorite outdoor job. Whenever she held a shiny red apple in her hand, she wished, oh, how she wished, she could take a big bite out of it! She longed to know if it tasted as good as it looked.

She didn't like the fact that she and the other slaves were expected to pick, wash, and polish these luscious-looking apples but were forbidden to eat any.

She didn't think it was fair that slaves did all the work and the family in the Big House got to eat the apples.

Each day as Harriet picked and polished apples, she looked for the chance to crunch into one.

One day when the overseer was walking down to the other end of the orchard, she thought, "This is my chance!"

But just as she was biting deep into a delicious apple, the overseer whirled around and caught her! Angrily, he took his whip and lashed Harriet. The whip tore through her clothing and into her flesh. It left scars that lasted the rest of her life.

She couldn't fight back or do anything about it then. But she made herself a promise. "One day I am going to be free—and I'm going to have all the apples I want."

Years passed, and Harriet married a free man by the name of John Tubman. In 1849, she learned that she might be sold and sent away from her husband and sisters and brothers. Harriet took action. She ran away from the Brodess plantation.

She walked until she reached a "safe house," a place where she knew members of the Underground Railroad would help her. (The Underground Railroad was not a railroad but a group of black and white men and women who took great risks to help people escape from slavery.)

Then, through dense forests and chilly swamps, she followed the North Star toward the North and freedom. She was always on the lookout for slave hunters and their bloodhound dogs.

Later Harriet was hidden in a farm wagon and taken to another safe house. Finally she reached the Delaware Bay in the state of Delaware. A boatman helped her cross to the New Jersey shore. From there she made her way to Philadelphia, Pennsylvania. Here in the North she was free, just as she had promised herself that she would be.

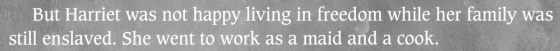

But Harriet was not happy living in freedom while her family was still enslaved. She went to work as a maid and a cook.

She saved her money and went back again and again to Maryland to free her family and lead many other people out of slavery.

It was extremely dangerous for Harriet to do this. There was a huge reward for her capture. The slaveholders were very angry that she had become an Underground Railroad "conductor"—guiding other slaves to freedom. But she and her "passengers" were never caught.

In 1869, Harriet bought a house near Auburn, New York.
She planted rows of apple trees along the lane that led from
the road to her home.

It had taken a long time, but she was finally able to keep
the second part of the promise she had made to herself.

Each fall when the apples were ripe and ready for picking, Harriet Tubman had all the apples she could eat—and she invited the townspeople to come and fill their baskets.

Harriet Tubman's apples were a symbol
of freedom for everyone to share.

AUTHOR'S NOTE

Harriet Tubman was the greatest "conductor" on the Underground Railroad. She made many trips into Southern states to free hundreds of enslaved Africans. She was called "Moses" because she led her people out of bondage.

When Harriet was born, her parents named her Araminta and called her "Minty." She later changed her name to Harriet. She was a Union army nurse and a scout during the Civil War. In just one day in June 1863, she led a raid that rescued seven hundred enslaved people.

Many books tell these facts and describe Harriet Tubman's heroism, but very few people know about her love of apples. I learned it during an interview in 1984 with her great-niece Mrs. Alice Brickler, who had learned it from Harriet Tubman herself. This story gives us new insight into the life of this remarkable heroine.

Harriet Tubman used to tell children, "Learn. Learn all you can. No one can take away what you have in your head." If you would like to find out more about her and about the Underground Railroad, you will enjoy reading:

> *Barefoot: Escape on the Underground Railroad*
> by Pamela Duncan Edwards (New York: HarperCollins, 1997).

> *If You Traveled on the Underground Railroad*
> by Ellen Levine (New York: Scholastic, 1993).

> *Journeys of Courage: On the Underground Railroad*
> by Darwin McBeth Walton with Glennette Tilley Turner
> (Orlando, Florida: Steck-Vaughn, 2003).

> *Minty: A Story of Young Harriet Tubman*
> by Alan Schroeder (New York: Dial Books for Young Readers, 1996).

> *Running for Our Lives*
> by Glennette Tilley Turner (Glen Ellyn, Illinois: Newman Educational Publishers, 2004).

> *Sweet Clara and the Freedom Quilt*
> by Deborah Hopkinson (New York: Knopf, 1993).

> *The Underground Railroad*
> by Raymond Bial (Boston: Houghton Mifflin, 1995).

Glennette Tilley Turner